DIY Bath Salts

A Step by Step Beginner's Guide to Making
Therapeutic and Natural Bath Salts

Sarah McMillan

Table of Contents

Introduction

I've always loved making things – from quilts to cozy winter scarfs, to homemade cookies, to wonderful concoctions meant to replace costly luxuries found at stores. Of all the crafts I enjoy making, bath salts are among the simplest yet they're also some of the most useful.

If you're like me, you probably love the concept of relaxing in a nice hot bath at the end of the day. And you've probably found yourself paying way too much for fancy, pre-packaged bath salts, too. But why spend so much money on something that's ultimately destined to go right down the drain? Once you learn how to make bath salts at home, you'll no longer have to waste money on pricey, prettily-packaged bath salts.

Making homemade bath salts takes very little time, and once you've purchased a few basic supplies, you'll discover that even the most luxurious bath salts recipes cost just a few cents per bath to make.

This book contains all the recipes you'll ever need to make bath salts for relaxation, as well as bath salts designed to help you get over common ailments faster and more comfortably. Besides getting all the information you need to confidently create wonderful bath salts for your own use, you'll learn some quick and easy ways to make and package bath salts intended for gift giving. If you're interested in treating your friends and family members to marvelous homemade gifts, you'll find that bath salts often serve as the perfect gift-giving solution.

Once you've made your first batch of bath salts, you'll be hooked – especially when you start counting up the savings. So, let's get started! We're about to delve a little deeper into the world of bath salts.

Chapter 1: Choosing Bath Salts: Healing Benefits and More

Bath salts have been used for centuries, not just by people looking for a relaxing escape from everyday drudgery, but by those looking for relief from common ailments such as arthritis, muscle pain, seasonal allergies, insomnia, colds, and the flu. Perhaps most important, bath salts help to cleanse and detoxify the body's largest organ – your skin.

The benefits of bath salts vary depending on the type of salt used, as well as on other ingredients used in formulating them. While the bath salts found on store shelves are often beneficial, homemade bath salts are even better. Why? Because it's completely up to you to customize them so you get the benefits you need most.

Making bath salts isn't a particularly scientific process; in fact, it is very simple. But to get the most from the bath salts you make, it's important to know a little bit about different kinds of salts and the benefits they provide.

Epsom Salt

Named in honor of the town of Epsom, in Surrey, England, Epsom salts were originally distilled from water obtained from springs located nearby. Today, there are many natural sources for the chemical compound magnesium sulfate. Composed of magnesium, oxygen, and sulfur, this compound forms tiny crystals that look very much like table salt. Though similar in appearance to the salt in your shaker, Epsom salts do not share healing properties with table salt.

The healing properties of Epsom salts are numerous. They include:

- Flushing toxins from the body

- Exfoliating and softening skin

- Relieving stress

- Relieving muscle pain and arthritis

- Preventing blood clots

Epsom salts are great for creating beneficial foot soaks and other beauty treatments. Be sure to experiment after you've gained experience with making your own bath salts.

Note that Epsom salt is not recommended for people with diabetes or high blood pressure, as it can aggravate health problems. Substitute another type of salt instead.

Dead Sea Salts

As their name implies, Dead Sea salts come from the Dead Sea, which is a salt lake that lies along the borders of Israel, the West Bank, and Jordan. Treasured for its therapeutic properties for thousands of years, the Dead Sea contains 27 percent salts in comparison with normal sea water, which is made up of three percent salts.

Chemically composted of potassium, magnesium, bromides, and calcium chloride, Dead Sea salts are unique among other natural salts, including those from seas and oceans and other salt lakes like Utah's Great Salt Lake. The main difference lies in the salt's magnesium chloride composition; other seas and inland salt lakes contain sodium chloride, which is the same component that makes up table salt.

Dead Sea salts offer a number of healing benefits that are directly related to the minerals they contain. These include:

- Magnesium – calms the nervous system, slows skin's aging process, and reduces fluid retention

- Potassium – balances skin's moisture while energizing the body

- Sodium – aids in balancing lymphatic fluid and strengthening the immune system

- Calcium – Strengthens body tissues including skin and nails; improves circulation

Dead Sea salt isn't just great for making homemade bath salts; it's also good for making salt scrubs, natural foot baths, and other wonderful spa goodies.

Himalayan Salt

Sourced from the high mountain ranges of the Himalayas and sometimes referred to as Jurassic Sea salt, Himalayan salt contains about 84 minerals and other elements that benefit the body. Formed millions of years ago and untouched by any of the toxins found in ocean salt, Himalayan Salt is very easy for the body to absorb.

The benefits of Himalayan salt are numerous and include:

- Reducing cramps

- Promoting healthy sleep

- Improving libido

- Improving circulation

- Reducing the outward signs of aging

- Promoting healthy pH balance throughout the body

- Encouraging balanced blood sugar

Himalayan salt has a lovely, natural pink color that makes it a wonderful choice for making bath salts for gift giving.

Atlantic Sea Salt

Atlantic sea salt is collected from some of the cleanest, deepest ocean waters in the world. Usually displaying a pure, white color and available in various crystal sizes, this type of bath salt is naturally absorbent and makes a great choice for adding color or scent to. Its benefits include:

- Promoting relaxation

- Detoxification

- Softening and cleansing skin

Mediterranean Sea Bath Salt

Harvested from the Mediterranean using a similar process to that used in collecting Atlantic sea salt, Mediterranean bath salt is sometimes referred to as European Spa bath salt. Widely used throughout Europe and the Mediterranean, this bath salt is typically available in a few different sized grains, with the larger grains being best for absorbing essential oils. Its benefits include:

- Aiding in effective exfoliation

- Improving circulation

- Promoting relaxation

Gray Bath Salt

Take a bath with gray salt? Give it a try! Grey bath salt is unwashed and unrefined. It is traditionally harvested in the Brittany region of France, and it contains large amounts of natural trace minerals that can enhance your health. Its benefits include:

- Nourishing skin

- Detoxification

- Balancing moisture

Hawaiian Red Bath Salt

If you want to create beautiful, colorful bath salts without adding coloring, consider giving Hawaiian red bath salt a try. Also known as Alaea sea salt or volcanic salt, it gets its distinctive color from red Hawaiian clay, which is naturally high in iron. Its benefits include:

- Aids in healing wounds

- Alleviates body aches

- Helps muscle sprains and strains heal faster

- Aids in detoxification

Sulfur Salt

Also known as Sanchal, Kala Namak, and Black Salt, sulfur salt has a pleasing pinkish-gray color that indicates its high mineral content. This type of bath salt comes from the volcanic regions of India and Pakistan, and is a staple used in a number of Ayurvedic healing treatments. Its benefits include:

- Purification

- Disinfecting

- Strengthening skin

- Promoting healing

Before investing in sulfur salt, it's important to note that this type of bath salt is sourced from sites where the same minerals that give sulfuric thermal springs their characteristic odor are found. You're likely to smell the distinctive scent during your bath, even when you add essential oils.

Where to Find Special Salts

You might have some Epsom salt already on hand, but the likelihood that you have any special salts lying around the house is low unless you've already been trying your hand at making your own bath salts.

It took some time for me to look into trying different salts, and once I did, I realized I should have made the effort earlier. Black salt, Himalayan salt, and even weird-looking gray sea salt are wonderful to keep on hand, thanks to their many wonderful healing properties. I encourage you to start off on the right foot by making a minor investment in at least a few different kinds of salts.

Some of these salts are available at brick and mortar shops including health food stores. If you can't find the salts you want locally, look for them online. There are a number of sites that specialize in selling different types of salts, and if you tend to take lots of baths and want to make a variety of recipes, you'll probably save quite a bit of money by purchasing salts online.

When looking for salts to use in the bath salts recipes in this book, don't worry about deviating slightly from the recipes I've created. You can mix different kinds of salts to create your own special blends, and you can often substitute one type of salt for another as long as you're aware that the recipe's therapeutic properties may change somewhat. Your baths will still be healthy and enjoyable, and you're likely to create some new favorites by experimenting.

Different Grains, Different Uses

When you buy commercially-produced bath salts, you're likely to see different grain sizes in different packages, particularly if you are purchasing high-end salts like the ones you'll be making yourself once you've learned a little more about formulating a variety of bath salts for different purposes.

Small grains that are about the same fineness as table salt or maybe a little coarser dissolve very quickly in water and are great for making salt scrubs that cleanse and exfoliate like nothing else. These grains will absorb fragrance, but are not capable of holding as much as larger grains. They are fantastic for blending with powdered herbs and other powdered ingredients.

Medium grains produce a nice product that typically looks attractive and dissolves fairly quickly. They are great for blending with larger bits of herb such as calendula or lavender buds, and they are capable of absorbing more fragrance and oil than smaller grains are.

Large grains absorb even more fragrance than medium grains, and they look beautiful when nicely packaged. These grains take longer to dissolve than smaller ones do, and you may find it easier to dissolve them in a bit of very hot water while drawing your bath, then adding the water to the bath so that you don't find yourself vying for space with the crystals slowly dissolving on the bottom of your tub.

Large Crystals or sea salt chunks are nice because they can be used several times before finally dissolving. After treating them with essential oils, consider placing them in a linen or organza bag with some herbs, hanging them from your bathtub's spout, and allowing the water to capture the blend's essence on its way into the tub.

Now that you're an expert on sea salts and other common types of bath salts, you're ready to learn a little more about some of the other ingredients you'll be using to create your own therapeutic blends.

Chapter 2: Bath Salts for Health and Healing: Choosing Quality Ingredients

Beyond choosing the best type of salt for the situation, the other ingredients you add to your bath salts make a difference. There's a vast amount of information available in books and online about the benefits of herbs and essential oils, and I encourage you to learn as much as you can so you don't have to learn by trial and error like I did. For the purposes of this book though, I'm focusing on presenting the "Reader's Digest" version in order to give you the most important facts about some of the best herbs and essential oils available. While you'll find that some of the bath salts recipes do call for other things, the majority of them make good use of herbs and/or essential oils.

Common Terminology

Before we dive into herbs and essential oils, let's take just a moment to go over some terminology that's commonly used to describe various properties associated with natural remedies. Don't worry – this will take just a minute and will help you create your own formulas later, if you want. Herbs and essential oils can have many other properties, but these are the ones that are most often associated with bath salts designed to help improve your health in some way.

Adaptogen: Adaptogens help to build up the immune system, and they increase the body's ability to tolerate stress. Bath salts containing adaptogenic herbs and essential oils are wonderful for bringing the body and mind into balance.

Analgesic: Analgesics are pain relievers. Headaches, lower back pain and muscle soreness, neuralgia, and other painful conditions are often alleviated with the help of bath salts containing analgesic herbs and essential oils.

Anti-inflammatory: Anti-inflammatory herbs and essential oils are good choices for all sorts of aches and pains. You might also find them useful if you're battling digestive issues.

Antibacterial: Antibacterial substances help the body to ward off infection. If you are suffering from a cold or the flu, or if you think you might have been exposed to a virus and you're hoping to stop it in its tracks before it has a chance to take hold, give antibacterial herbs and essential oils a try.

Antidepressant: Antidepressant herbs and essential oils aren't normally used to replace prescriptions, but they can work wonders for lifting your mood in the event you find yourself in a funk. Mental stress, grief, anger, and other tough emotions can be alleviated with the help of bath salts that contain natural antidepressants.

Antifungal: Let's face it: fungus is everywhere. If you're suffering from a case of athlete's foot, candida, or ringworm you picked up while out and about, antifungal herbs and essential oils can help. Choose an antifungal bath salts recipe and bathe in it at least once a day while using other, complementary remedies to eradicate fungus faster.

Diuretic: Many of the bath salts we talked about in the previous chapter have diuretic properties, meaning they help to remove excess water from the body's system, bringing it back into balance. Adding diuretic herbs or essential oils to a bath salts recipe can make it even more effective. If you've overdone it and want to ward off the uncomfortable feelings of puffiness and bloating that come along with excess water weight, give these remarkable remedies a try.

Emmenagogue: Herbs and essential oils that help stimulate menstrual flow are called emmenagogues. Using an emmenagogue can help restore your cycle to normal, and it can sometimes help in dealing with painful periods. One very important note: do not use bath salts containing emmenagogues if you are pregnant.

Emmolient: Emmolient herbs and essential oils help to soften, smooth, and soothe the skin. Bath salts containing emmolients are helpful anytime, but are particularly useful for healing dry, irritated skin.

Expectorant: Herbs and essential oils with expectorant properties help to loosen congestion and clear the lungs. If you're suffering from sinusitis, seasonal allergies, bronchitis, a cold, or any other uncomfortable health problem that involves congestion, using bath salts containing expectorant herbs or essential oils can be of great help.

Sedative: Just like pharmaceutical sedatives, herbs and essential oils with sedative properties can calm and relax the body and mind. These won't normally knock you out like a prescription sleep aid will; instead, they help you relax and unwind so you drift effortlessly off to sleep.

Herbs: The Basics

When you think of herbs, your thoughts might immediately spring to the kitchen spice cabinet where things like cinnamon, thyme, oregano, and cloves are found. You're on the right track! Many of the same herbs we use to make food taste better have some therapeutic qualities that make them great additions to bath salts. Some others have nice fragrances that relax or energize the mind, making baths even more enjoyable as well as more useful.

Some of the ingredients I discuss while talking about herbs aren't traditional, leafy green herbs in the botanical sense. Instead, they are plant parts or plant-based derivatives that can make your bath salts more enjoyable and effective.

There are hundreds of medicinal plants and herbs including many that I never knew much about before I became interested in making my own bath salts, and covering all of them here would require hundreds of additional pages. If you're interested in using a certain herb you don't see listed below, go ahead and give it a try! Just be sure to look into safety before giving these helpful, natural remedies a go. You can find herbs online and at health food stores, and many are very easy to grow in your own garden.

Essential Oils: What You Need to Know

Essential oils impart delightful fragrances to bath salts, but that's not all they do. Made by distilling the stems, leaves, bark, flowers, roots, and other plant components, essential oils are extremely concentrated so that even a drop or two goes a long way. It takes about 4,000 pounds of roses to produce a single pound of rose essential oil, meaning that every drop contains the power of several whole plants. There's no way you could bathe in a tub filled with that many flowers; there'd be no room for you!

So called because they contain the true essences of the plants from which they are derived, essential oils are treasured for their therapeutic value. They contain the same healing molecules whole plants and herbs contain, but in a highly concentrated form that makes them perfect for addition to bath salts. Even when highly diluted, essential oils are readily absorbed into the skin, and when added to hot water, the molecules drift up on the steam and can be inhaled into the lungs, where they enter the body's bloodstream and provide therapeutic benefits.

Single essential oils have specific benefits, and blended essential oils can be of great use as well. Entire books have been written about the benefits of essential oils, and there are hundreds of single oils and blends to try.

Now that you know a little more about essential oils, you might be wondering where to find them. Almost all health food stores carry a nice selection of the most popular essential oils, and some grocery stores carry them as well. I like to buy mine locally when possible, but I find that I often get better prices online. When deciding which essential oils to buy for use in bath salts and other remedies, be sure that you choose those offered for sale by reputable companies. You can learn more by reading reviews and checking out the company's philosophy on its website.

When shopping, be sure that you choose essential oils, not fragrance oils. These are not the same, and while they might smell delightful, they don't offer the same therapeutic benefits essential oils do. This being said, here are fifteen top essential oils to try. Note that several recipes do call for essential oils I haven't covered here, but also note that those oils are easy to find and aren't among the ones that come with extensive safety warnings.

Clary Sage – Clary sage essential oil is an outstanding antidepressant that can also help to relieve anxiety. Its benefits don't stop with your mind, however; it's the number one essential oil for soothing menstrual issues as well as for helping to relieve uncomfortably menopause and pre-menopause symptoms. Because it helps to relax nerve impulses, it's also a great choice for dealing with headaches, coughs, muscle cramps, and other pain naturally.

Clary sage essential oil is a potent antibacterial and antifungal agent as well. It's a good addition to bath salts meant for warding off common illnesses such as colds and the flu, and its astringent properties make it a wonderful choice for toning skin and hair.

Because clary sage is a potent emmenagogue, it shouldn't be used by women who are pregnant or nursing.

Eucalyptus – If you're suffering from a cold or the flu, give eucalyptus essential oil a try. Whether blended with other essential oils or used in bath salts on its own, it's the perfect choice for clearing sinuses and improving breathing naturally. It also stimulates the body's immune response, helping you to get over minor illnesses faster.

Eucalyptus essential oil is great for including in blends meant to soothe aches and pains, and it can help stop the sting of insect bites and skin infections, too. If you have a minor burn or blisters, using eucalyptus bath salts can help bring relief and healing.

If you suffer from high blood pressure or epilepsy, stay away from eucalyptus essential oil. Also, this is not a good choice for women who are pregnant or nursing.

Frankincense – With its wonderful fragrance and its ability to improve a wide range of skin conditions, frankincense essential oil is an excellent choice for creating irresistible bath salts you'll enjoy using anytime you feel the need to relax and let go of your worries.

Frankincense essential oil helps to tone and balance the entire body, benefits all the body's systems, and encourages healing. It is also an excellent choice for mental relaxation, as it promotes a sense of peaceful calm when inhaled. In the event you are suffering from grief or anxiety, you'll find that treating yourself with some simple frankincense bath salts can be very helpful.

Ginger – Feeling nauseous? Ginger essential oil can help. It's also beneficial to anyone suffering from heartburn, and it is a good choice for pregnant women looking to quell the effects of morning sickness. Its sweet, spicy aroma makes it a pleasure to use, and it blends very well with a number of other essential oils.

Helichrysum – Helichrysum essential oil has long been treasured for its ability to smooth and soften skin, as well as for its ability to help alleviate a number of skin conditions. It is a great choice for use in bath salts recipes meant stop the itchiness of fungal or bacterial skin conditions, and it's perfect for including in recipes for soothing the sting of insect bites and the pain of sunburn.

You may also find that helichrysum essential oil helps with cold and flu symptoms, and if you suffer from seasonal allergies, it can help provide some natural, non-invasive relief.

Lavender – Lavender essential oil is my go-to for bath salt blends meant to enhance feelings of relaxation and well-being. It's perfect for a bedtime bath – so much so, that I use it more than any other essential oil. It is the perfect adaptogen, meaning you can use it to help bring balance back to your body and mind any time you're feeling a little off-kilter.

Not only does lavender essential oil help send you off to dreamland, it's a great choice for promoting healing. If you are suffering from minor skin irritation, bruises, or a rash, you will find that bath salts made with lavender essential oil can help.

When you're feeling stressed, anxious, frustrated, or angry, lavender can help. Be sure to breathe deeply while you're soaking to experience the full relaxing power this wonderful essential oil has to offer.

Lemon – With its fresh, clean scent, lemon essential oil is a wonderful choice for using in bath salts meant to help refresh and energize the body and mind. But its ability to invoke feelings of happy invigoration isn't all that this delightful essential oil is known for; it's also great for the skin.

If you are suffering from acne or another common skin ailment, you'll find that bath salts made with lemon essential oil can be a huge help due to the oil's strong antiseptic quality.

Lemon essential oil is also an excellent choice for toning, balancing, and rejuvenating skin in general, as it stimulates lymphatic flow and helps to remove toxins. If you're working to banish cellulite, you'll find that adding baths made with lemon essential oil to your regimen can help.

When fighting a cold, the flu, or another viral issue, you'll find that blending bath salts with lemon essential oil and soaking until the water cools can be a great help. Because this essential oil is high in antiviral compounds, it can help to shorten the duration of many common ailments.

Mandarin – Not only does mandarin essential oil have an irresistible fragrance that uplifts the spirits almost instantly, it's also a valuable antiseptic with a number of other useful qualities. If you're picking out just one or two essential oils to begin with, you might want to make this one of them!

Like lemon and other citrus essential oils, mandarin is a great choice for including in bath salts that are meant to help shorten colds, ease coughing, and put a stop to other symptoms associated with common illnesses. Because it acts against muscle spasms, it is also a great choice for using in blends for soothing sore muscles, cramps, and general inflammation.

Mandarin essential oil is valued for its ability to help purify the body, and in addition to acting as a powerful detoxification agent, it helps to promote healthy cellular growth. Perhaps best of all, you can use it any time you're feeling a little under the weather to give your entire immune system a boost.

Neroli – Neroli essential oil has a lovely, sensual fragrance that makes it perfect for including in bath salts meant to stimulate your romantic side. It is also an excellent choice for calming frazzled nerves and bringing on a sense of total well-being. Considered to be among the world's top natural antidepressants, this essential oil helps to promote feelings of relaxation and happiness.

Not only is neroli essential oil an excellent choice for improving mental health naturally, it's also a great essential oil to add to your arsenal of skin treatments. Adding it to bath salts can help balance the skin and impart faster healing in cases of irritation.

Patchouli – Not only does patchouli essential oil impart a wonderfully spicy fragrance to bath salts, it's a great choice for boosting your mood naturally. Its constituents stimulate the release of dopamine, serotonin, and other pleasure hormones, helping feelings of anger, sadness, and anxiety disappear.

Patchouli essential oil also soothes inflammation, and its antiseptic property makes it a good choice for inclusion in blends meant to aid in healing. It is also a cicatrisant, meaning that it can help old scars fade over time. At the same time, patchouli essential oil is a cytophylactic, meaning it helps to stimulate the growth of new cells. Used regularly, it can help regenerate your skin for a healthy, vibrant look and feel.

This essential oil is a potent diuretic, and not only will it help you get rid of excess water weight, it might help you curb your appetite. It also helps boost metabolism, making it the perfect choice for anyone who wants to lose a bit of weight.

Peppermint – Not only does peppermint essential oil smell fantastic, it's an excellent choice to include in bath salts for alleviating common problems like nausea, headaches, and muscle soreness.

Peppermint essential oil is also a great choice for including in bath salt recipes intended for use during cold season. It helps to improve the body's immune response, aids in clearing the respiratory tract, and provides mild pain relief.

In the event you need a mental pick-me-up, the idea of taking a relaxing soak might seem counterintuitive. In most cases, this is true; but the scent of peppermint essential oil stimulates mental activity and taking a "breather" while inhaling deeply can really help to reinvigorate and refresh the mind while alleviating stress, restlessness, and anxiety – all things that can prevent your mind from doing its best work.

Roman Chamomile – Roman chamomile essential oil is a nice one to keep on hand for making bedtime bath salts, and it's also useful for making blends designed to target feelings of restlessness and anxiety.

Not only can bath salts made with Roman chamomile essential oil help to soothe the mind, they can soothe and heal irritated skin, especially in cases of sunburn and windburn. If you suffer from eczema, psoriasis, or hemorrhoids, you may find Roman chamomile helpful.

In the event you can't find Roman chamomile essential oil but you see German essential oil for sale, feel free to pick it up and use it. While a little less potent than its cousin, it is still an effective remedy and a great addition to relaxing bath salts.

Rosemary – Rosemary essential oil is linked to improved memory, but that's not all this wonderful, natural remedy is useful for. Add rosemary essential oil to bath salts to reduce pain, relieve respiratory issues during cold and allergy season, and tone your skin.

This essential oil stimulates circulation and is a wonderful choice for including in detoxification blends, and its antiseptic and antimicrobial qualities make it a great essential oil for using in blends to relieve the symptoms of various types of dermatitis including acne, oily skin, and eczema. If your goal is healthy, glowing skin, do not miss out on the benefits of rosemary!

Rosemary essential oil decreases cortisol levels, making it a very good addition to relaxing bath salts. If you suffer from chronic stress, using blends made with rosemary can help your body battle its harmful effects while helping to restore a sense of overall balance.

Using bath salts made with rosemary essential oil also gives your immune system a boost, helping to ward off colds and the flu. These bath salts are also great for soothing various aches and pains, all while imparting a lovely fragrance.

Rose Geranium – If you're hoping to improve the overall condition of your skin while fighting the signs of aging, make yourself some bath salts with rose geranium essential oil. Not only will you enjoy the strong, rosy fragrance this essential oil offers, you'll emerge from the bath with beautifully glowing skin. Used regularly, this essential oil can make a major difference in the way your skin looks and feels.

Not only does rose geranium essential oil help improve skin, it promotes greater creativity and imparts a sense of energy while relieving tension. You can use it in bedtime blends to promote pleasant dreams or enjoy it anytime you need to take a break.

Tea Tree – With its strong, pungent scent, tea tree essential oil is a favorite for creating medicinal bath salts that help stop cold and flu symptoms and much, much more. Tea tree essential oil is renowned for its ability to help promote overall healing, stop itching, and eliminate fungal problems such as athletes' foot. Because it also boosts immunity, it is a great choice for using any time.

If you're suffering from congestion, add tea tree essential oil to bath salts and inhale deeply while relaxing. Whether you've got a cold, bronchitis, or seasonal allergies, you'll find that this remedy really helps.

In the event you feel as though you're sweating more than usual while taking a bath made with tea tree essential oil, take this as a sign that the oil is working deep within your body to help effect healing. This essential oil is a strong sudorific, meaning it promotes perspiration to help remove toxins, clean the pores, and balance the body.

Herbs and essential oils offer a natural, beneficial way to add fragrance to bath salts recipes. Now that you know more about them, it's time to start making enjoyable bath time concoctions of your own.

Chapter 3: Above Average Bath Salts: 40 Simple Recipes

A Quick, Foolproof Guide to Making Bath Salts

Making homemade bath salts isn't at all difficult, and in the event you're missing one of the ingredients a certain recipe calls for, you can very easily substitute it with something else or even leave it out altogether.

Unless you are making colored bath salts with different layers of colors, the basic method for blending your bath salts is rarely going to vary. Some books call for mixing bath salts in a bowl, but in most cases, I find that's not necessary. On the other hand, if you're making a large batch of bath salts, you might want to use a bowl and double, triple, or even quadruple the ingredients, blend everything together, and then pour the mixture into jars, using a funnel to avoid spills.

Some recipes call for dried herbs, flowers, and other "messy" ingredients that add to the bath salt's aesthetic appearance. These don't add as much fragrance as essential oils do, but once added to hot bath water, they release their healthful constituents, adding to the overall efficacy of the bath salts. You can omit them if you like, or you can cut down on the messiness by placing them in a clean, dry blender or food processer and grinding them up first. Your bath salts won't look as pretty, but they'll be almost as enjoyable to use and you'll have a little less cleanup to deal with after bathing.

The Basic Process for Making Bath Salts

Before you get started, be sure that all of the tools – the bowls, jars, spoons, and other items – you plan to use are clean and completely dry. Water won't ruin your bath salts, but the finished results won't be as nice if they are contaminated with moisture.

Start by blending all of the dry ingredients together. If you're using your hands to do this, be sure to wear a disposable glove, as the salt will draw the moisture from your skin and could cause dryness.

The next step is to add dyes and oils. Blend well here, stirring slowly but thoroughly to keep the crystals intact and ensure that all the ingredients you've added are completely incorporated.

Many bath salts recipes completely avoid the use of carrier oils such as almond, sunflower, or olive oil, partly because these can leach through to the bottom of the jar. I have tried making my bath salts without carrier oil, and with a couple of exceptions, I find I prefer them with oil added. If you don't like the idea of using oil, go ahead and leave it out of your recipes. If you want more oil, add it! If you don't have the recommended type of oil on hand, go ahead and use it.

A quick note about dyes – play with colors if you like, but be careful when making layered blends. I tried a rainbow bath salts recipe that turned my bathwater brown – not very appetizing! I decided to include just one layered recipe in this chapter. If you decide to layer, use colors that complement one another so you don't end up with the same unappetizing problem I faced.

Once you've blended your bath salts and capped them, it's time to make your containers look nice – or at least label them so you remember what's inside. You'll find a complete guide to creating beautiful packages in the next chapter.

Ready? You're about to become an expert at making your own bath salts.

Bath Salts Recipes

Alluring Almond Bath Salts

Almond oil softens even the driest skin, leaving it feeling wonderfully smooth. Add a few drops extra to your bath for even more softening power.

Ingredients

- 1 cup gray bath salts

- 2 tablespoons sunflower or almond oil

- 4 drops frankincense essential oil

Instructions, Tips, and Considerations

Combine all ingredients in a glass container with a tight fitting lid. Stir gently until oils have been absorbed.

Use two to four tablespoons of bath salts for each tubful of water, stirring the salts before measuring to ensure they reabsorb any oil that might have leached out into the bottom of the jar.

This recipe makes excellent use of gray bath salts and frankincense essential oil, both of which are favorites due to their ability to improve skin's texture. Note that you can replace the gray bath salts with another type if you like, and you can use any kind of essential oil you happen to enjoy.

Buttermilk Bath Salts

Because it is rich in lactic acid, buttermilk is an excellent natural exfoliant that helps to soften and brighten skin. If you're suffering from dryness, these bath salts will help. Use them at least three times weekly for best results.

Ingredients

- 2 cups Gray sea salt

- 2 cups buttermilk powder

- 20 drops helichrysum essential oil

Instructions, Tips, and Considerations

Combine all ingredients in a glass container with a tight fitting lid. Stir gently until oils have been absorbed.

Use ¼ cup of bath salts for each tubful of warm water, and spend at least twenty minutes in the tub for best results. Follow up with your favorite lotion.

Note that you can make some substitutions. Gray salt is rich in minerals and great for skin, but if you can't find it, go for Mediterranean sea salt or Dead Sea salt if possible. Helichrysum essential oil is particularly nice for keeping skin looking its best, however you can use any kind of essential oil you like and still enjoy the many wonderful benefits of buttermilk.

Christmas Tree Bath Salts

Pine essential oil doesn't just smell fantastic, it also has an uplifting effect on the spirits. It also helps ease cold and flu symptoms, so be sure to enjoy a soak in this bath even if it's not quite Christmas.

Ingredients

- 1 cup gray bath salt
- 1 tablespoon olive oil
- 10 drops pine essential oil
- 1 drop peppermint essential oil

Instructions, Tips, and Considerations

Combine all ingredients in a glass container with a tight fitting lid. Stir gently until oils have been absorbed.

Use two to four tablespoons of bath salts for each tubful of water, stirring the salts before measuring to ensure they reabsorb any oil that might have leached out into the bottom of the jar.

A fun bath salts recipe with layered colors that will remind you of a summer sunset, these bath salts have a lovely citrus fragrance anyone will enjoy.

Ingredients

- 2 cups sea salt

- 1 cup baking soda

- 3 teaspoons sunflower or almond oil

- 10 drops mandarin essential oil

- 5 drops lemon essential oil

- 5 drops sweet orange essential oil

- 2 drops yellow food or soap coloring

- 2 drops orange food or soap coloring

- 2 drops red food or soap coloring

Instructions, Tips, and Considerations

In a large bowl, combine the sea salt and baking soda. Add the sunflower or almond oil, stirring well to ensure that it is evenly distributed, then add the essential oils.

Divide the salts evenly into three smaller bowls. Add the yellow dye to one bowl, the orange dye to the second bowl, and the red dye to the third bowl. Add more color if you don't feel the colors are bright enough, and consider trying out your own blends of yellow, red, and orange to achieve different hues.

Once you're satisfied with the colors, layer small amounts of the bath salts into decorative jars with tight-fitting lids.

Use two to four tablespoons of bath salts for each tubful of water. This is a fun recipe for kids to use, although it's not suitable for anyone under four years old.

Cooling Mojito Bath Salts

If you've ever enjoyed a mint mojito on a hot summer day, you know just how refreshing the combination of fresh lime and mint can be. Because this recipe calls for fresh lime juice, you'll need to use it right away.

Ingredients

- 4 tablespoons Epsom salt

- 1 tablespoon sunflower or almond oil

- Juice from one lime

- 2 drops peppermint essential oil

- 1 drop green food or soap coloring (optional)

Instructions, Tips, and Considerations

Combine all ingredients in a small bowl. Don't worry if the salt begins to dissolve; you'll receive its full benefits once this blend has been added to a warm bath.

Use the entire recipe in the tub, and try to remain there until the water has completely cooled. You'll emerge feeling wonderfully refreshed.

Rosemary, peppermint, and sage come together in this recipe to open blocked sinuses and help alleviate the discomfort that comes with a cold or the flu.

Ingredients

- 1 cup Himalayan salt

- 1 tablespoon olive oil

- 2 drops sage essential oil

- 2 drops rosemary essential oil

- 1 drop peppermint essential oil

Instructions, Tips, and Considerations

Combine all ingredients in a glass container with a tight fitting lid. Stir gently until oils have been absorbed.

Use two to four tablespoons of bath salts for each tubful of water, stirring the salts before measuring to ensure they reabsorb any oil that might have leached out into the bottom of the jar.

If you have a little extra time, dissolve your dose of bath salts in boiling water before adding them to the bath. Be sure that the boiling water doesn't make your bath too hot to handle, and enjoy the vapors as you breathe deep.

Creative Inspiration Bath Salts

Stuck in a rut? Need to find a solution to one of life's problems or work on a creative endeavor of some kind? Vanilla helps inspire creativity, while sandalwood helps to ease tension and stimulate positive thinking. Be sure to use natural vanilla extract in this recipe, and consider blending about a teaspoon of real vanilla into your favorite unscented lotion, which you can apply after bathing to keep the flow of creative thoughts going.

Ingredients

- 2 cups Himalayan salt

- 1 tablespoon vanilla extract

- 2 teaspoons sunflower or almond oil

- 10 drops sandalwood essential oil

- Contents of one vanilla bean (optional)

Instructions, Tips, and Considerations

Place the Himalayan salt in a bowl and add the vanilla extract, stirring until it has been absorbed. Add the sunflower or almond oil and stir it in, then add the sandalwood essential oil and the vanilla bean seeds. Stir again before using a funnel to pour the bath salts into a glass jar with a tight-fitting lid.

Use two to four tablespoons of bath salts for each tubful of water, stirring the salts before measuring to ensure they reabsorb any oil that might have leached out into the bottom of the jar, and start out with a bath as hot as you can stand to ensure the vanilla and sandalwood fragrance completely envelopes you. Breathe deeply, relax, and let your thoughts flow!

If you're suffering from the flu or just feeling under the weather, these bath salts can help. Don't miss out by skipping this recipe in the event you have no ginger essential oil on hand; just double up on the amount of ground ginger you add to the blend.

Ingredients

- 1 cup Epsom salt

- ½ cup baking soda

- 2 tablespoons ground ginger

- 2 tablespoons sunflower or almond oil

- 4 drops ginger essential oil

Instructions, Tips, and Considerations

Combine all ingredients in a glass container with a tight fitting lid. Stir gently until oils have been absorbed.

Use two to four tablespoons of bath salts for each tubful of water, stirring the salts before measuring to ensure they reabsorb any oil that might have leached out into the bottom of the jar.

Be sure that you are well-hydrated before you use this blend, and ensure that your bathwater is hot enough to promote sweating, and try to stay in the tub for at least 20 minutes, submerging as much of your body as you can. Stay hydrated by enjoying a cup of tea or drinking water while relaxing in the tub. Continue to consume clear liquids for at least an hour after bathing.

Note that the ground ginger is likely to cling to your body. While it won't harm you and will come off on your towel, you can avoid messiness by rinsing off under a warm shower after you've finished soaking.

Grapefruit essential oil is an excellent natural remedy for detoxification. If you've overdone it in some way or are doing a whole-body cleanse, be sure to give this recipe a try.

Ingredients

- 1 cup Dead Sea salts

- 6 drops grapefruit essential oil

- 1 tablespoon olive oil

Instructions, Tips, and Considerations

Combine all ingredients in a glass container with a tight fitting lid. Stir gently until oils have been absorbed.

Use two to four tablespoons of bath salts for each tubful of water, stirring the salts before measuring to ensure they reabsorb any oil that might have leached out into the bottom of the jar.

Be sure to stay in the bath for at least 20 minutes, inhaling deeply as you relax.

Refresh body, mind, and spirit with these wonderfully refreshing bath salts. The combination of rosemary, eucalyptus, and peppermint essential oils is a truly energizing one. Though you'll feel relaxed while bathing, you will emerge from the bath with a renewed sense of purpose.

Ingredients

- 1 cup Epsom salt

- 2 cups Pacific Sea salt

- 3 tablespoons olive oil

- 5 drops eucalyptus essential oil

- 11 drops rosemary essential oil

- 14 drops peppermint essential oil

- 2 drops blue food or soap coloring (optional)

Instructions, Tips, and Considerations

Combine all ingredients in a glass container with a tight fitting lid. Stir gently until oils have been absorbed.

Use two to four tablespoons of bath salts for each tubful of water, stirring the salts before measuring to ensure they reabsorb any oil that might have leached out into the bottom of the jar.

If planning to make a big batch of these bath salts for gift giving, consider adding about ¼ cup crushed mint and about a tablespoon of finely chopped rosemary leaves to the blend to give it a pleasing appearance.

Make these bath salts before cold season arrives so you have them on hand when you need them. The combination of the eucalyptus and tea tree essential oils is a powerful one, helping to clear sinuses while combating the viruses that cause these common illnesses.

Ingredients

- 2 cups Epsom salt

- 2 cups gray salt

- 2 cups baking soda

- 2 tablespoons sunflower or olive oil

- 20 drops eucalyptus essential oil

- 20 drops tea tree essential oil

- 10 drops pine essential oil (optional)

- 5 drops peppermint essential oil (optional)

- 2 drops blue food or soap coloring (optional)

- 1 drop green food or soap coloring (optional)

Instructions, Tips, and Considerations

Combine the Epsom salt, gray salt, and baking soda in a large glass or metal bowl, then add the sunflower or olive oil, mixing until the oil has been absorbed. Add the essential oils and the colorings, then stir again until all ingredients have been absorbed.

Use a funnel to pour the bath salts into glass containers with tight fitting lids. Pour any oil that may have leached out into the containers as well.

Use two to four tablespoons of bath salts for each tubful of water, stirring the salts before measuring to ensure they reabsorb any oil that might have leached out into the bottom of the jar.

If you've got some time to make a bit of a mess and slough off dead skin, give this fantastic exfoliating bath salts recipe a try. Be sure to bring a soft bath brush into the tub with you to make it easier to access hard to reach places.

Ingredients

- 1 cup gray bath salt

- 2 cups Himalayan salt

- 1 cup rolled outs, blended into a rough powder

- 5 drops mandarin essential oil

Instructions, Tips, and Considerations

Combine all ingredients in a glass container with a tight fitting lid. Stir gently until essential oil has been absorbed.

Use 1 cup of bath salts for each tubful of water, and soak for 30 minutes or until the water cools. Give your body a thorough scrubbing before you stand up, then take a warm shower. Apply your favorite body lotion afterward and enjoy the feeling of soft, smooth skin.

Note that the mandarin essential oil is just a suggestion – it is a nice, uplifting fragrance that most people enjoy. You can use any fragrance you like in this blend!

A wonderful blend for gift giving and a great one for enjoying during the holidays, these beautiful bath salts look fantastic when presented in pretty jars.

Ingredients

- 1 cup sea salt

- 1 cup Epsom salt

- ½ cup baking soda

- 5 drops cedar essential oil

- 5 drops pine essential oil

- 5 drops fir essential oil

- Contents of one green tea teabag

- 2 tablespoons pine needles

- 2 tablespoons dried juniper berries

Instructions, Tips, and Considerations

Combine all ingredients in a glass container with a tight fitting lid. Stir gently until oils have been absorbed.

Use two to four tablespoons of bath salts for each tubful of water, stirring the salts before measuring to ensure they reabsorb any oil that might have leached out into the bottom of the jar.

Note that the tea, pine needles, and juniper berries can leave a bit of a mess in the bathtub. Omit them if you like, or fill an organdy bag with two tablespoons of the bath salts mixture prior to bathing. Toss the entire bag into your bath and allow the salts to dissolve. Discard the bag's contents after bathing.

Relax and unwind as you enjoy the beautiful fragrance of a meadow in summer. This blend is fantastic as is, but don't miss out if you don't have one of the essential oils on hand. It's great even with just two of the four.

Ingredients

- 1 cup sea salt

- 1 tablespoon sunflower or almond oil

- 6 drops geranium essential oil

- 6 drops rose essential oil

- 6 drops lavender essential oil

- 1 drop sandalwood essential oil

Instructions, Tips, and Considerations

Combine all ingredients in a glass container with a tight fitting lid. Stir gently until oils have been absorbed.

Use two to four tablespoons of bath salts for each tubful of water, stirring the salts before measuring to ensure they reabsorb any oil that might have leached out into the bottom of the jar.

Both frankincense and myrrh essential oils are great for skin, and the fragrance these beautiful oils create when combined is absolutely magnificent.

Ingredients

- 1 cup Dead Sea salt

- 1 tablespoon olive oil

- 3 drops frankincense essential oil

- 3 drops myrrh essential oil

Instructions, Tips, and Considerations

Combine all ingredients in a glass container with a tight fitting lid. Stir gently until oils have been absorbed.

Use two to four tablespoons of bath salts for each tubful of water, stirring the salts before measuring to ensure they reabsorb any oil that might have leached out into the bottom of the jar. Start out with a very hot bath to completely envelope yourself in the fragrance and reap all its aromatherapy benefits.

When suffering from the stress of PMS or the symptoms of menopause, let these lovely green goddess bath salts ease your body and mind. With clary sage essential oil, which is renowned for its ability to encourage deep relaxation, this recipe is one you'll want to keep on hand for dealing with other stressful situations as well.

Ingredients

- 2 cups Himalayan salt

- 2 tablespoons sunflower or almond oil

- 15 drops clary sage essential oil

- 5 drops jasmine essential oil or 5 drops frankincense essential oil

- 2 drops blue food or soap coloring (optional)

- 1 drop green food or soap coloring (optional)

Instructions, Tips, and Considerations

Combine all ingredients in a glass container with a tight fitting lid. Stir gently until oils have been absorbed.

Use two to four tablespoons of bath salts for each tubful of water, stirring the salts before measuring to ensure they reabsorb any oil that might have leached out into the bottom of the jar.

Note that while clary sage essential oil is often used to relax women who are in labor, those who are pregnant and not ready to deliver should not use it.

Chamomile essential oil has a gentle scent that will help you feel good, and adding some dried chamomile flowers to the blend gives it a beautiful, natural look.

Ingredients

- 2 Cups Himalayan bath salts

- 2 tablespoons sunflower or almond oil

- 10 drops chamomile essential oil

- ¼ cup crushed chamomile flowers

Instructions, Tips, and Considerations

Combine all ingredients in a glass container with a tight fitting lid. Stir gently until oils have been absorbed.

Use two to four tablespoons of bath salts for each tubful of water, stirring the salts before measuring to ensure they reabsorb any oil that might have leached out into the bottom of the jar.

Note that the crushed chamomile flowers can leave a bit of a mess in the bathtub. Omit them if you like, or fill an organdy bag with two tablespoons of the bath salts mixture prior to bathing. Toss the entire bag into your bath and allow the salts to dissolve. Discard the used chamomile flowers after bathing.

Whether celebrating Christmas or another holiday, you'll enjoy this wonderfully fragrant blend. Be sure to package it prettily if presenting it to friends!

Ingredients

- 2 cups fine sea salt

- 2 tablespoons sunflower, almond, or olive oil

- 1 tablespoon ground cinnamon

- 1 tablespoon ground ginger

- 1 tablespoon ground nutmeg

- 3 drops red food coloring (optional)

Instructions, Tips, and Considerations

If using food coloring, blend it with the sea salt before adding the spices. Add the spices and stir well, then place the bath salts into a glass container with a tight-fitting lid.

Use two to four tablespoons of bath salts for each tubful of water, and shower quickly after bathing to rinse off any spices that might be clinging to your skin.

Tea tree essential oil is one you can use for all kinds of things including wonderful, cleansing bath salts, and when combined with lavender, is wonderfully restorative. This recipe will make a difference when you're under the weather.

Ingredients

- ½ cup Epsom salt

- ½ cup Dead Sea salt

- 2 cups Atlantic Sea salt

- 20 drops lavender essential oil

- 20 drops tea tree essential oil

Instructions, Tips, and Considerations

Combine all ingredients in a bowl, mix until oils have been absorbed, then transfer to a glass container with a tight fitting lid.

Use two to four tablespoons of bath salts for each tubful of water, stirring the salts before measuring to ensure they reabsorb any oil that might have leached out into the bottom of the jar.

This recipe doesn't have any oil in it as it makes a huge quantity that will stay fresh for over a year when kept in a cool, dark place. If you'd like to moisturize while bathing, add a teaspoon or two of your favorite oil to the bath at the same time as you add the bath salts.

With a beautiful fragrance and a delightful appearance, these herbal bath salts make a fantastic gift – just be sure that you make enough for yourself to enjoy as well.

Ingredients

- 2 cups Dead Sea salt

- 2 cups baking soda

- 4 tablespoons sunflower, almond, or olive oil

- 6 drops lemon essential oil

- 3 drops basil essential oil

- 4 tablespoons finely chopped rosemary leaves

- 4 tablespoons crushed dried basil

- 4 tablespoons dried lemon zest

Instructions, Tips, and Considerations

Combine all ingredients in a glass container with a tight fitting lid. Stir gently until oils have been absorbed.

Use two to four tablespoons of bath salts for each tubful of water, stirring the salts before measuring to ensure they reabsorb any oil that might have leached out into the bottom of the jar.

Because the dried herbs and lemon zest are likely to cling to your skin, you'll find it helpful to shower off after bathing. Alternately, you can or fill an organdy bag with two tablespoons of the bath salts mixture prior to bathing. Toss the entire bag into your bath and allow the salts to dissolve. Discard the used herbs after bathing.

With a fragrance that's at once woody, spicy, and just a little sweet, these invigorating basil-bergamot bath salts serve as a wonderful pick-me-up. Enjoy them anytime you need a little inspiration.

Ingredients

- 1 cup Epsom salt

- 2 drops basil essential oil

- 2 drops cypress essential oil

- 3 drops bergamot essential oil

- 1 tablespoon olive oil

- 1 drop blue food or soap coloring (optional)

- 1 drop green food or soap coloring (optional)

Instructions, Tips, and Considerations

Combine all ingredients in a glass container with a tight fitting lid. Stir gently until oils have been absorbed.

Use two to four tablespoons of bath salts for each tubful of water, stirring the salts before measuring to ensure they reabsorb any oil that might have leached out into the bottom of the jar.

Both lavender and peppermint are renowned for their ability to lift the spirits and help ease the pain caused by tension headaches. Give yourself at least half an hour of quiet time during which to enjoy this bath.

Ingredients

- 1 cup Mediterranean Sea salt

- 1 tablespoon sunflower or almond oil

- 3 drops lavender essential oil

- 2 drops peppermint essential oil

Instructions, Tips, and Considerations

Combine all ingredients in a glass container with a tight fitting lid. Stir gently until oils have been absorbed.

Use two to four tablespoons of bath salts for each tubful of water, stirring the salts before measuring to ensure they reabsorb any oil that might have leached out into the bottom of the jar.

While this recipe calls for Mediterranean Sea salt due to its relaxing properties, any type of bath salt will work.

Patchouli, cypress, and vetiver essential oils come together in this bath salts recipe, helping you to relax, clear your mind, and place your focus inward. Enjoy them at the beginning or end of your day, ensuring you breathe deep throughout your bath.

Ingredients

- 2 cups Himalayan salt

- 2 tablespoons almond or sunflower oil

- 20 drops patchouli essential oil

- 10 drops vetiver essential oil

- 10 drops cypress essential oil

Instructions, Tips, and Considerations

Combine all ingredients in a glass container with a tight fitting lid. Stir gently until oils have been absorbed.

Use two to four tablespoons of bath salts for each tubful of water, stirring the salts before measuring to ensure they reabsorb any oil that might have leached out into the bottom of the jar.

If you love the fragrance of patchouli, you'll enjoy using these bath salts. Patchouli essential oil isn't just great for your skin, it has a subtly aphrodisiac effect and is wonderful for using anytime you have romance on your mind. If you're feeling meditative, this is a great recipe to use, as patchouli is also renowned for its ability to facilitate meditation. It's also a good choice for easing stress and promoting deep sleep.

Ingredients

- ½ cup Epsom salt

- ½ cup Himalayan salt

- 1 cup baking soda

- 2 teaspoons almond or sunflower oil

- 20 drops patchouli essential oil

- 1 drop green food or soap coloring (optional)

Instructions, Tips, and Considerations

Combine all ingredients in a glass container with a tight fitting lid, first mixing the salts and baking soda together, then adding the remainder of the ingredients. Stir gently until oils have been absorbed.

Use two to four tablespoons of bath salts for each tubful of water, stirring the salts before measuring to ensure they reabsorb any oil that might have leached out into the bottom of the jar.

Peppermint, spearmint, and eucalyptus essential oils come together to give these bath salts a wonderfully uplifting fragrance that will help you regain your sense of enthusiasm during stressful times. If you have no spearmint or eucalyptus essential oils on hand, double the amount of peppermint and enjoy the sensation.

Ingredients

- 1 cup Epsom salt

- 1 cup Dead Sea salt

- 1 cup baking soda

- 3 tablespoons sunflower or almond oil

- 6 drops peppermint essential oil

- 6 drops spearmint essential oil

- 3 drops eucalyptus essential oil

- 3 drops green food or soap coloring (optional)

- 3 tablespoons dried mint, crushed (optional)

Instructions, Tips, and Considerations

Combine the Epsom salt, Dead Sea salt, and baking soda in a large bowl, stirring well. Add the sunflower or almond oil, blending well to ensure it is evenly distributed, then add the remainder of the ingredients, stirring gently to ensure that all oil is absorbed.

Use a funnel to transfer the bath salts to a glass container with a tight-fitting lid. Pour any oil remaining in the bowl into the container with the bath salts.

Use two to four tablespoons of bath salts for each tubful of water, stirring the salts before measuring to ensure they reabsorb any oil that might have leached out into the bottom of the jar.

Note that the crushed mint can leave a bit of a mess in the bathtub. Omit it if you like, or fill an organdy bag with two tablespoons of the bath salts mixture prior to bathing. Toss the entire bag into your bath and allow the salts to dissolve. Discard the mint after bathing.

A wonderful soak that will leave you feeling fresh and clean while alleviating sinus trouble, these eucalyptus bath salts are very simple but effective.

Ingredients

- 1 cup Atlantic sea salt

- ½ cup baking soda

- 1 tablespoon sunflower or almond oil

- 4 drops eucalyptus essential oil

- 1 drop green food or soap coloring (optional)

Instructions, Tips, and Considerations

Combine all ingredients in a glass container with a tight fitting lid. Stir gently until oils have been absorbed.

Use two to four tablespoons of bath salts for each tubful of water, stirring the salts before measuring to ensure they reabsorb any oil that might have leached out into the bottom of the jar.

If packaging this recipe for gift giving, consider using raffia to tie a sprig of eucalyptus to the outside of the jar.

Ease back pain and other muscle aches with this fragrant, relaxing blend of essential oils and Epsom salt. Skip any ingredients you don't have on hand; while the bath works best when it contains all the elements listed, it will be helpful even when one or two are missing.

Ingredients

- 1 cup Epsom salt

- ½ cup baking soda

- 1 tablespoon sunflower or almond oil

- 6 drops peppermint essential oil

- 3 drops rosemary essential oil

- 3 drops cinnamon essential oil

- 3 drops eucalyptus essential oil

- 3 drops lavender essential oil

- 2 tablespoons crushed lavender flowers (optional)

- 2 tablespoons crushed fresh rosemary leaves (optional)

Instructions, Tips, and Considerations

Combine all ingredients in a glass container with a tight fitting lid. Stir gently until oils have been absorbed.

Use two to four tablespoons of bath salts for each tubful of water, stirring the salts before measuring to ensure they reabsorb any oil that might have leached out into the bottom of the jar. Ensure that your bath is as hot as you can stand it, and try to stay in the water for at least twenty minutes.

Note that the crushed lavender flowers and rosemary leaves can make a mess in the bathtub and stick to your body. Omit them if you like, or fill an organdy bag with two tablespoons of the bath salts mixture prior to bathing. Toss the entire bag into your bath and allow the salts to dissolve. Discard the used lavender flowers and rosemary leaves after bathing.

Rosemary essential oil has an amazingly transformative effect on the mind. If you're feeling mentally exhausted and need to forge ahead instead of calling it a day, use these bath salts to feel better.

Ingredients

- 1 Cup Himalayan salt

- 1 Cup gray bath salt

- 2 tablespoons olive oil

- 20 drops rosemary essential oil

- ½ cup chopped, dried rosemary leaves

Instructions, Tips, and Considerations

Combine all ingredients in a glass container with a tight fitting lid. Stir gently until oils have been absorbed.

Use two to four tablespoons of bath salts for each tubful of water, stirring the salts before measuring to ensure they reabsorb any oil that might have leached out into the bottom of the jar.

Note that the dried rosemary leaves can stick to you and leave a mess in the bathtub. Omit them if you like, or fill an organdy bag with two tablespoons of the bath salts mixture prior to bathing. Toss the entire bag into your bath and allow the salts to dissolve. Discard the rosemary leaves after bathing.

The powdered milk in this recipe helps soften skin, while the rose essential oil provides a beautiful, relaxing fragrance. Try rose geranium essential oil if you have no rose available.

Ingredients

- 1 cup full-fat powdered milk

- ½ cup Epsom salt

- 2 drops rose essential oil

- ¼ cup dried rose petals (optional)

Instructions, Tips, and Considerations

Combine the powdered milk and Epsom salt in a bowl, stirring until fully incorporated. Add the essential oil, stirring with a fork to ensure that there are no lumps. Add the rose petals. Store in a glass container with a tight fitting lid.

Use about ½ cup of bath salts for each tubful of water, stirring well before you get into the tub. Remove any rose petals that are clinging to your skin by showering off after finishing with your bath.

Boost your immune system and help remove toxins by bathing with these bath salts daily when colds and the flu are making their rounds. Double or triple the recipe if you plan to share with friends or family members.

Ingredients

- 2 cups Epsom salt

- 1 cup Himalayan salt

- 3 tablespoons baking soda

- 3 tablespoons sunflower or almond oil

- 12 drops rosemary essential oil

Instructions, Tips, and Considerations

Combine all ingredients in a wide-mouth quart canning jar with a tight fitting lid. Stir gently until oils have been absorbed.

Use two to four tablespoons of bath salts for each tubful of water, stirring the salts before measuring to ensure they reabsorb any oil that might have leached out into the bottom of the jar.

Sensual Ylang-ylang Bath Salts

Ylang-ylang essential oil is well-known for its usefulness as a natural aphrodisiac, and its delicate fragrance delights the senses even when a romantic evening isn't in the cards.

Ingredients

- 1 cup Epsom salt

- 2 cups Himalayan bath salts

- 10 drops ylang-ylang essential oil

- 3 tablespoons sunflower or almond oil

- 1 drop red food or soap coloring (optional)

Instructions, Tips, and Considerations

Combine all ingredients in a glass container with a tight fitting lid. Stir gently until oils have been absorbed.

Use two to four tablespoons of bath salts for each tubful of water, stirring the salts before measuring to ensure they reabsorb any oil that might have leached out into the bottom of the jar.

Instead of taking sleeping pills, treat yourself to a soothing bedtime bath. This blend is marvellously relaxing, and will send you off to sleep in comfort and peace.

Ingredients

- 1 cup Epsom salt

- 1 tablespoon sunflower or almond oil

- 8 drops lavender essential oil

- 3 drops ylang-ylang essential oil

Instructions, Tips, and Considerations

Combine all ingredients in a glass container with a tight fitting lid. Stir gently until oils have been absorbed.

Use two to four tablespoons of bath salts for each tubful of water, stirring the salts before measuring to ensure they reabsorb any oil that might have leached out into the bottom of the jar.

Get better sleep by taking care of everything you need to do before taking this bath. That way, you can simply slip into bed after bathing, toweling off, and applying a bit of your favorite lotion.

Soothing Jasmine Bath Salts

When you're feeling stressed, jasmine essential oil can make a difference. This recipe makes enough bath salts to keep on hand for those times when you really need to relax.

Ingredients

- 2 cups Epsom salts

- 2 tablespoons sunflower or almond oil

- 12 drops jasmine essential oil

Instructions, Tips, and Considerations

Combine all ingredients in a glass container with a tight fitting lid. Stir gently until oils have been absorbed.

Use two to four tablespoons of bath salts for each tubful of water, stirring the salts before measuring to ensure they reabsorb any oil that might have leached out into the bottom of the jar.

Note that you can use any kind of natural, moisturizing oil to make this recipe. Sweet almond oil is my favorite because its fragrance doesn't compete with the jasmine.

Perfect for relaxing after a long, hard day, these soothing lavender bath salts contain both essential oil and natural lavender flowers. Double or triple the recipe to ensure you always have some on hand.

Ingredients

- 1 cup Epsom salts

- 1 tablespoon sunflower or almond oil

- 5 drops lavender essential oil

- 1 drop purple food or soap coloring (optional)

- 1 tablespoon crushed lavender flowers

Instructions, Tips, and Considerations

Combine everything but the crushed lavender flowers in a glass container with a tight fitting lid. Stir gently until oils have been absorbed. Add the lavender flowers and stir again before closing the lid tightly.

Use two to four tablespoons of bath salts for each tubful of water, stirring the salts before measuring to ensure they reabsorb any oil that might have leached out into the bottom of the jar.

Note that the crushed lavender flowers can leave a bit of a mess in the bathtub. Omit them if you like, or fill an organdy bag with two tablespoons of the bath salts mixture prior to bathing. Toss the entire bag into your bath and allow the salts to dissolve. Discard the used lavender flowers after bathing.

Spiced Orange Bath Salts

This sumptuous blend makes a nice substitute for dessert. Savor the fragrance as you relax and unwind.

Ingredients

- 1 cup Himalayan salt

- 1 tablespoon sunflower or almond oil

- 6 drops sweet orange essential oil

- 1 drop clove essential oil

- 1 drop ginger essential oil

- 1 tablespoon finely grated orange rind

Instructions, Tips, and Considerations

Combine all ingredients in a glass container with a tight fitting lid. Stir gently until oils have been absorbed.

Use two to four tablespoons of bath salts for each tubful of water, stirring the salts before measuring to ensure they reabsorb any oil that might have leached out into the bottom of the jar.

Note that the grated orange rind can leave a bit of a mess in the bathtub. Omit it if you like, or fill an organdy bag with two tablespoons of the bath salts mixture prior to bathing. Toss the entire bag into your bath and allow the salts to dissolve. Discard the rind after bathing.

If you're feeling itchy due to a healing sunburn, insect bites, or even a mild case of poison ivy, you'll find that these bath salts help bring immediate relief. Don't skip the oatmeal in this recipe as it is particularly soothing to itchy skin.

Ingredients

- 1 cup Himalayan salt

- 1 cup baking soda

- 1 cup rolled oats ground into a fine powder

- Contents of three chamomile teabags

- 15 drops chamomile essential oil

Instructions, Tips, and Considerations

Start by using your food processer or blender to grind the oats into a fine powder. If you'd like to skip this step, you can purchase some 100 percent oat flour instead.

In a large bowl, combine the oats with the Himalayan salt and baking soda. Add the chamomile tea and the essential oil, stirring gently until the essential oil has been absorbed.

Use ¼ cup of bath salts for each tubful of warm water, stirring the salts before measuring to ensure they reabsorb any oil that might have leached out into the bottom of the jar.

Note that this recipe will bring relief, but that like commercial anti-itch baths containing oatmeal, it is messy. Shower in lightly warm water after bathing, then pat yourself dry. Apply calamine lotion or another anti-itch remedy after drying off, and repeat the entire process once or twice daily until the rash is gone.

Summer Sunrise Bath Salts

Wake up with the fantastic fragrances of mandarin and lime. This blend is sure to help you start your day out right!

Ingredients

- 2 cups Himalayan salt

- 2 tablespoons sweet almond oil

- 10 drops mandarin essential oil

- 4 drops lime essential oil

Instructions, Tips, and Considerations

Combine all ingredients in a glass container with a tight fitting lid. Stir gently until oils have been absorbed.

Use two to four tablespoons of bath salts for each tubful of water, stirring the salts before measuring to ensure they reabsorb any oil that might have leached out into the bottom of the jar.

With ground oatmeal to soothe skin, plus bergamot and sweet orange to ease tension, this marvelous blend also includes cypress essential oil, which alleviates stress while nourishing skin.

Ingredients

- 1 cup Himalayan salt

- ¼ cup rolled oats, ground

- 4 drops bergamot essential oil

- 2 drops sweet orange essential oil

- 2 drops cypress essential oil

Instructions, Tips, and Considerations

Combine the ground oats and salt in a glass container with a tight fitting lid, then add the essential oils. Stir gently until oils have been absorbed.

Use two to four tablespoons of bath salts for each tubful of water, stirring the salts before measuring to ensure they reabsorb any oil that might have leached out into the bottom of the jar.

Note that this recipe doesn't contain any oil other than the essential oils, since it can combine with the oats and cause lumps. If you'd like to add moisture to your bath, use a teaspoon of your favorite oil to the bathtub after stirring in the bath salts.

When you've had a rough day, nothing quite compares to a relaxing bath made with a blend of essential oils and other ingredients meant to help you unwind. Give this recipe a try, and don't be surprised if it ends up becoming a favorite.

Ingredients

- ½ cup Epsom salt

- ½ cup Gray salt or Mediterranean Sea salt

- 1 cup baking soda

- 1 tablespoon sunflower or almond oil

- 5 drops sandalwood essential oil

- 5 drops rosemary essential oil

- 6 drops patchouli essential oil

- 1 drop blue food or soap coloring (optional)

- 1 tablespoon finely chopped rosemary leaves (optional)

- 1 tablespoon dried lavender flowers (optional)

- 1 tablespoon dried chamomile flowers (optional)

Instructions, Tips, and Considerations

Combine the Epsom salt, gray or Mediterranean Sea salt, and baking soda in a bowl, stirring well. Add the sunflower or almond oil, incorporating thoroughly, and then add the remainder of the ingredients, stirring until all the oils have been absorbed. Use a funnel to pour the bath salts into a glass container with a tight-fitting lid.

Use two to four tablespoons of bath salts for each tubful of water, stirring the salts before measuring to ensure they reabsorb any oil that might have leached out into the bottom of the jar.

Note that the dried leaves and flowers can leave a bit of a mess in the bathtub. Omit them if you like, or fill an organdy bag with two tablespoons of the bath salts mixture prior to bathing. Toss the entire bag into your bath and allow the salts to dissolve. Discard the organic materials after bathing.

Uplifting Mandarin-Lemon Bath Salts

If you're feeling stressed and a little depressed, enjoy a soak with these uplifting bath salts. Both lemon and mandarin essential oils have the amazing ability to make you feel more positive. Be sure you inhale deeply while bathing.

Ingredients

- 1 cup Himalayan salt

- 2 drops lemon essential oil

- 5 drops mandarin essential oil

- 1 tablespoon almond oil

- 1 tablespoon finely grated lemon peel (optional)

- 1 tablespoon finely chopped rosemary leaves (optional)

Instructions, Tips, and Considerations

Combine all ingredients in a glass container with a tight fitting lid. Stir gently until oils have been absorbed.

Use two to four tablespoons of bath salts for each tubful of water, stirring the salts before measuring to ensure they reabsorb any oil that might have leached out into the bottom of the jar.

Note that the grated lemon peel and chopped rosemary leaves do contribute to the therapeutic quality of these bath salts, and that they make the blend look fantastic, particularly if you're planning to give these salts as a gift. These ingredients can leave a bit of a mess in the bathtub, however. Omit them if you like, or fill an organdy bag with two tablespoons of the bath salts mixture prior to bathing. Toss the entire bag into your bath and allow the salts to dissolve. Discard the used lemon peel and rosemary leaves after bathing.

Chapter 4: Inexpensive, Yet Elegant: Bath Salts for Gift Giving

Who doesn't love a fragrant, relaxing bath? Bath salts make fantastic gifts for just about everyone on your list and for nearly any occasion. They're inexpensive to make, particularly if you buy ingredients in bulk, and they are fun to personalize with beautiful packaging.

Who Wants Bath Salts?

Moms, sisters, cousins, aunts, and nieces – just about everyone loves bath salts! If you find yourself in need of a simple, inexpensive gift for a teacher or neighbor, a pretty jar of homemade bath salts could be exactly the solution you're looking for.

Choosing the Best Containers for Your Bath Salts

Package your bath salts in pretty or interesting containers to add a special spa-like feel to the gifts you're giving. Be creative and infuse the gift with personality, and people will appreciate the gifts even more. Sure, it takes a little extra effort to find the right containers for the bath salts you make, but the end results are fantastic.

Jam and jelly jars with two-piece lids are inexpensive and can be purchased in bulk. They're very easy to dress up with ribbons, decorations, and tags, and they come in a variety of different shapes and sizes. You can find a wealth of information on dressing up mason jars online, with ideas for painting them, and applying special finishes so they look like miniature works of art that people will be proud to display near their tubs.

Flip-cap glass water bottles have an elegant appearance and are very nice for packaging large quantities of bath salts. You can purchase them at some craft stores as well as from online retailers, and you may be able to find them in interesting colors. Some beverages still come in bottles with flip tops, and so long as you wash and dry the bottles after enjoying the beverages, they make great upcycled containers.

Flip-cap jars with rubber seals are a great-looking choice for packaging your bath salts, and because they come in different shapes, colors, and sizes, personalization is very easy. If you want to add a splash of color to your bath salts but don't like the idea of using food or soap coloring, packaging the salts in a colored glass container is a great alternative.

Milk bottles are fantastic for packaging bath salts, and so are the smaller milk-bottle shaped jars that are available at craft stores and websites that specialize in crafting materials. Be sure to purchase corks to fit the jars you buy if they're not included.

Wine bottles make great containers for bath salts. Just be sure to remove the labels and consider purchasing new corks at a craft store. Ensure you wash and dry repurposed wine bottles thoroughly before refilling them with bath salts.

Small glass bottles in interesting shapes are also ideal for packaging bath salts. Many come with interesting stoppers, and colors like blue, aqua, green, and purple add extra visual appeal.

Sugar shakers, which are very easy to find at retailers that carry housewares, make fantastic bath salts containers as they have handy built-in spouts that make pouring the salts into the bath simple. Place a small piece of tape over the spout to prevent spills if using this type of jar and packaging it for gift giving.

Tins also make good containers for bath salts; package the salts in plastic bags before placing them in the tin to ensure that they do not react with the metal.

Labels

If making just one or two jars of bath salts to present as gifts, handwritten labels made with a permanent marker that won't stain the recipient's skin will probably do, but if you're making lots of bath salts, consider making pre-printed labels to apply to the jars.

Visit a craft store or office supplies store, and you'll find all sorts of fantastic labels including styles specifically designed for various holidays and attractive all-purpose designs that can be used for just about any occasion.

Decorations and Accessories

Here's where you get to show off your creative skills! Ribbons, twine, raffia, and different types of colored cord or yarn can be used to tie all sorts of things to the bottles and jars you've packaged your bath salts in. Some ideas:

- Paper tags containing bath salts information

- Christmas ornaments

- Pine cones

- Autumn leaves

- Seashells

- Whole, dried herbs

- Silk flowers

- Small wood or metal scoops

Making Spa Packages and Other Considerations

If you want to make the gift of homemade bath salts even more special, why not create an entire spa package? Bath bombs, body lotions, and other potions make great additions to a gift basket or bag packed with a few different types of bath salts, as do candles, pedicure supplies, and other thoughtful yet inexpensive goodies. Packaged in a pretty tin, basket, or gift bag, they are certain to be appreciated.

You don't need a lot of time to make bath salts for gifts – in fact, you can whip up a batch within about ten minutes so long as you have the necessary ingredients on hand. Be sure to try the bath salts you plan to make for gift giving on yourself before making a large batch to package up as gifts. You might find that you want to add a little more or less of a certain essential oil, and you may find that you like some of the recipes better with a little color added or perhaps with no color at all. Test your recipes by making about a fourth of a batch – just enough for one or two baths. This way, you'll have a better idea about whether the intended recipient will enjoy the as is, or slightly modified.

Keep in mind that people with diabetes and high blood pressure should not use Epsom salt, and substitute another type of salt if you're not sure whether any of your gift recipients have one of these health issues.

Conclusion

You don't have to spend big bucks to pamper yourself, and when it comes to gift giving, there's no need to break the bank. With DIY bath salts, you have the ability to improve your mood, ease pain, relax, and so much more.

I encourage you to get started with your first batch of bath salts right away. The recipes in this book are very easy to use, and because they can be modified to suit your needs and work with a variety of ingredients, they can be made any time. When you find a recipe you like, make a little extra to keep on hand. You never know when you'll need it.

It is my hope that you have enjoyed this book and that you will enjoy all of the recipes it contains. There are so many to try, you'll soon find yourself looking for an excuse to hide away in the bath. With bath salts, every bathing experience is like a mini-vacation. Enjoy!